TURKEY VULTURE

Samantha Kohn

A Crabtree Crown Book

Crabtree Publishing

crabtreebooks.com

T0014876

School-to-Home Support for Caregivers and Teachers

This appealing book is designed to teach students about core subject areas. Students will build upon what they already know about the subject, and engage in topics that they want to learn more about. Here are a few guiding questions to help readers build their comprehension skills. Possible answers appear here in red.

Before Reading:

What do I know about turkey vultures?

- *I know that a turkey vulture is a type of bird.*
- *I know that turkey vultures have bald heads.*

What do I want to learn about this topic?

- *I want to know where in the world turkey vultures are found.*
- *I want to learn about how turkey vultures grow and change.*

During Reading:

I'm curious to know...

- *I'm curious to know why turkey vultures migrate.*
- *I'm curious to know how turkey vultures are related to storks.*

How is this like something I already know?

- *I know that some birds are scavengers and eat dead animals.*
- *I know that birds use their beaks for different purposes.*

After Reading:

What was the author trying to teach me?

- *The author was trying to teach me about the turkey vulture's unique characteristics.*
- *The author was trying to teach me about how the turkey vulture compares to other birds.*

How did the images and captions help me understand more?

- *The labels on the picture of the turkey vulture pointed out its physical characteristics.*
- *The pictures showed me about the types of plants and animals in the turkey vulture's habitat.*

Contents

Meet the Turkey Vulture

When you think of a turkey, do you think of a yummy holiday meal? Don't think of turkey vultures when Thanksgiving comes around—they're not turkeys at all! People just called them turkey vultures because their red heads and brown bodies reminded them of turkeys.

WHO AM I?

Turkey vultures are part of the *Cathartidae* family of vultures and condors. You might also hear people call them a buzzard or carrion crow. Scientists call them a *cathartes aura*.

FIVE FABULOUS TURKEY VULTURE FACTS

1. Turkey vultures have featherless heads.
2. They eat carrion, or the flesh of dead animals.
3. Snacking on the dead can be a dirty business. A turkey vulture's bald head helps make sure dinner does not get stuck to any feathers.
4. Turkey vultures are great at hiding things. They lay their eggs in caves, **crevices**, hollowed out trees, or even in abandoned buildings.
5. In the wild, turkey vultures live for around 16 years. This vulture's bright red head and "socks" shows that it is a **mature** bird.

Ahem...attention bird lovers!
I am Professor Oddfeather and I will be your
expert guide to the fine feathered friend featured in this book.
I will direct you to amusing facts on odd birds. They really are the
most amazing creatures on Earth. I say this because I am one.
Seriously, I'm a living dinosaur! Look for my instructive
comments throughout the book.

Spot the Turkey Vulture

Shh...if you're quiet, you could spot a turkey vulture up in a tree in the early morning, catching some rays with its wings spread out. This helps it warm up after a cool night.

A turkey vulture's eyesight and sense of smell are incredible! They can find **carcasses** from one mile (1.6 km) away, even when they're up in the air!

Check out this curved, sharp beak. It is so powerful that it can rip through thick leather just as easily as you can tear a piece of paper!

These folds are called **lappets**. They serve no purpose other than to help make the turkey vulture an odd-looking bird!

Despite their large size, turkey vultures weigh only around four pounds (1.8 kg)—about the same as a large soda bottle!

Only adult turkey vultures have bald, bright red heads. Young turkey vultures have dark gray heads.

6

There are about 4.5 million turkey vultures in the world. They all live in North and South America.

Breeding season

Year round

Mature turkey vultures are 24 to 31 inches (60 to 80 cm) long, with a wingspan of 70 inches (170 cm).

Most **birds of prey** use their sharp talons to cut their food. Turkey vultures, on the other hand, use their beaks. Their skinny, chicken-like feet don't "cut it!"

Where in the World?

Did you know there are 23 species of vultures in the world? There are New World vultures and Old World vultures.

Turkey Vultures are New World vultures. They are related to storks. There are seven different species of New World vultures, including the huge California Condor.

Old World vultures are related to eagles. There are 16 species of Old World vultures. They are mostly named for the way they look, such as the red-headed or white-headed vulture (right).

Vultures of the World

New World vultures live in North and South America, while Old World vultures live in Africa, Europe, and Asia.

New World **range**   Old World range

Here are some key similarities and differences between New World and Old World vultures.

	Old World Vultures	New World Vultures
Both Old World and New World vultures have large wingspans that help them soar in search of meals.	✓	✓
All vultures are **scavengers**. That means they eat animals that are already dead.	✓	✓
Old World vultures have strong legs and feet with sharp talons. These are good for tearing apart flesh. New World vultures have thin feet, so they use their sharp beaks to eat instead.		
All vultures have strong stomachs that produce acids that allow them to eat rotting flesh.	✓	✓
Old World vultures are born with voice boxes. New World vultures do not have voice boxes, so they can only hiss and grunt.		
Old World vultures build nests to keep their eggs safe, while New World vultures find hiding spots for their eggs in crevices or hollowed-out trees.		

Meet the Family

The easiest way to tell New World vultures apart is by looking at their heads. Here's how a turkey vulture's head compares with the heads of other New World vultures.

Turkey Vulture
- Bald, bright red heads on adults; juvenile heads are dark gray
- Sharp, pale, curved beaks
- Black and dark brown feathers on body

Black Vulture
- Bald head with gray, wrinkly skin
- Strange eyelashes, with one row on the top eyelid and two rows on the bottom
- Glossy, black-feathered body

King Vulture

- Bald head with skin that can be yellow, orange, blue, purple, red, or any combination!
- Flashy caruncle on the beak
- Mostly white body with a gray tail, **ruff**, and light feathers

California Condor

- Babies have a gray head, but the color gets brighter with age
- Adult California Condors have pink, yellow, or orange skin on their big, bald heads
- Body is covered in black feathers with fluffy, long feathers around the neck

Andean Condor

- Bald head that's usually a dull, reddish color
- Adult males have a caruncle on their heads
- Body is black with a ruff of white feathers around the neck

Caruncles are fleshy growths on a bird's head, like you see here. They're usually bright and very easy to see! This muscovy duck is not a vulture, though. He is just visiting.

Superstar Skills

Vultures are scavengers. That may sound like an insult, but it's not! Scavengers serve a very important purpose. Turkey vultures use all their incredible skills and senses to survive.

FLYING AND SOARING
Turkey vultures can travel up to 200 miles (322 km) a day.

AIR? WHO NEEDS IT?
These birds' heart and lung systems allow them to fly up to 20,000 feet (6,096 m).

SMELL YOU ~~LATER~~ SOONER
Turkey vultures can sniff out a meal within 12 to 24 hours of an animal's death.

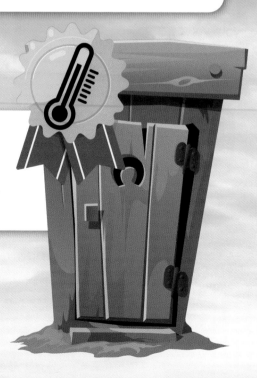

HEY, AHHH COOL!
On a hot day, most birds will cool off in a pond or puddle. Not turkey vultures! They pee on their own legs to cool off.

Scientists call this urohidrosis.

Marabou stork
13 feet (3.96 m)

Great white pelican
12.1 feet (3.7 m)

Trumpeter swan
10 feet (3 m)

Turkey vulture
6 feet (1.8 m)

Black crow
4 feet (1.2 m)

American robin
9 inches (22 cm)

Bee hummingbird
2 inches (5.5 cm)

The wingspan in flying animals is measured to the tips of the longest primary feathers.

What's for Dinner?

We know that turkey vultures eat carrion. But that's not the grossest part. When a turkey vulture finds the dead meat, it feeds by opening the animal with its sharp beak and sticking its head right inside! Good thing these scavenging birds are bald! Imagine the mess!

SMELLS DELICIOUS
Many birds do not have a strong sense of smell—but the turkey vulture is a big exception! They have the sharpest sense of smell of any bird. That's because their **olfactory system** is the largest of all birds.

MENU

APPETIZER

ENTRÉE

DESSERT

A turkey vulture's large nostrils can detect a tiny whiff of delicious carrion in the air. Mmmmm!

ON THE MENU
Turkey vultures aren't picky. They will eat meat that is easily available to them, from tiny rodents to huge whale carcasses. Though they mostly chow down on mammals, turkey vultures will also eat reptiles, fish, other birds, and insects. How does a grasshopper appetizer, raccoon entrée, and turtle dessert sound?

ENVIRONMENTAL HEROES!
While their choice of meal is pretty yucky, it's very helpful for the environment. By eating carrion before it rots, turkey vultures help take harmful **toxins** out of the environment.

Decomposer (vulture, insects, fungi)

Producer (grass)

Primary consumer (mouse)

PART OF A SYSTEM
Energy moves within an ecosystem. Producers make food for themselves and other living things. Consumers eat other living things. Decomposers break down dead organisms. Scavengers are a type of decomposer.

Tertiary consumer (fox)

Secondary consumer (snake)

Turkey vultures like their meat fresh. If it's more than a day or two old, they won't even eat it!

Roadkill Kings

You've probably heard the term roadkill...the animals you see on the side of the road that died being hit by a car. Roadkill may not look delicious to you, but it's a turkey vulture's favorite snack!

AN EASY MEAL
Turkey vultures have been on Earth way longer than cars—and roadkill—have. So how did it become a favorite snack for these scavengers? Turns out, they will always prefer an easy meal. Roadkill is easy to find and does not require the turkey vulture to hunt. Win-win!

Though they prefer hunting for fresh meat, coyotes will munch on any food available to them, including roadkill.

CLEAN-UP CREW
Spot some turkey vultures circling in the sky? They may be getting ready to clean up some roadkill nearby. But vultures aren't nature's only roadside cleaners.

A bear's excellent sense of smell allows it to detect rotting meat from over two miles (3.2 km) away.

Komodo dragons are **apex predators**. They hunt all kinds of **prey**, but will also feast on easy meals of delicious roadkill.

Roadkill on the dinner table? Sounds gross, but eating roadkill safely can be a way to **salvage** meat. Eating roadkill is legal in some states and provinces.

Small, black carrion beetles, as their name suggests, eat all kinds of dead animals.

Black vultures often take advantage of the turkey vulture's ability to find a roadkill meal. They stay close so that when a turkey vulture finds a snack, they can swoop in and steal it!

On the Wing

Turkey vultures live in North and South America, but they don't always stay in the same place! Turkey vulture **migrations** start in September. The distance a turkey vulture travels depends on where it started out.

Turkey vultures love to travel. They are the most migratory of all vultures!

Turkey vultures in the Northeast—think Ontario, New York, and Michigan—take small trips down to places like North Carolina and Louisiana.

Turkey vultures living in Western areas, like Oregon and California, prefer to spend their winters in the warm South—sometimes all the way down to Venezuela and Ecuador!

Alaska (USA)

Canada

USA

Mexico

18

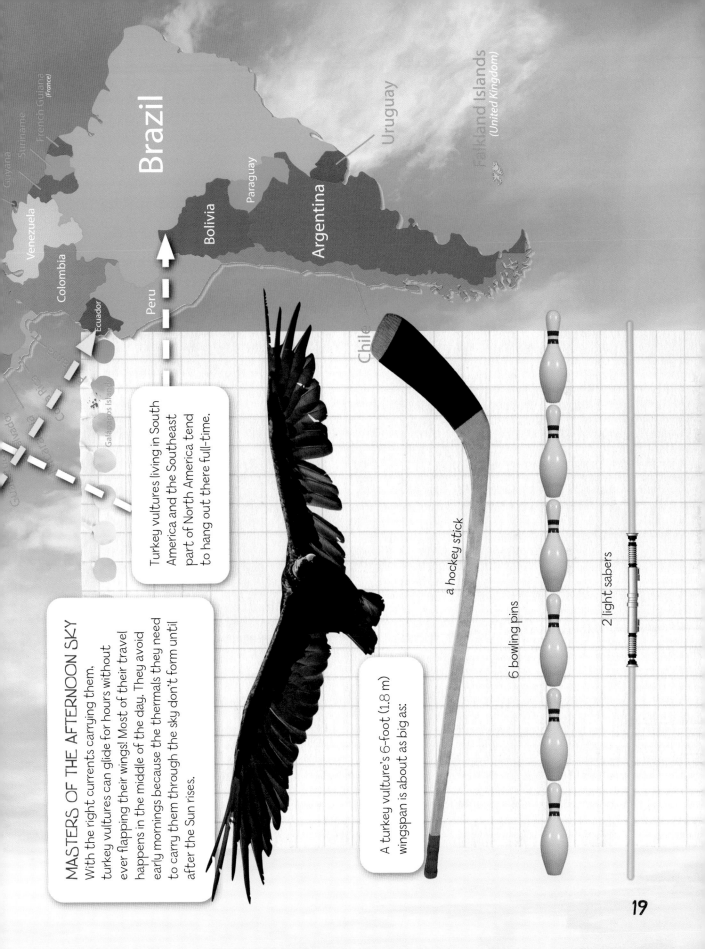

MASTERS OF THE AFTERNOON SKY

With the right currents carrying them, turkey vultures can glide for hours without ever flapping their wings! Most of their travel happens in the middle of the day. They avoid early mornings because the thermals they need to carry them through the sky don't form until after the Sun rises.

Turkey vultures living in South America and the Southeast part of North America tend to hang out there full-time.

A turkey vulture's 6-foot (1.8 m) wingspan is about as big as:

a hockey stick

6 bowling pins

2 light sabers

Brazil

Guyana

Suriname

French Guiana *(France)*

Venezuela

Colombia

Ecuador

Galápagos Islands

Peru

Bolivia

Paraguay

Argentina

Uruguay

Chile

Falkland Islands *(United Kingdom)*

Hanging with the Chicks

Turkey vultures are tough! They don't need a soft, cushy bed to lay their eggs...just a good hiding spot!

TIME TO NEST
Turkey vultures don't build nests high in trees. Instead, they gather up plant matter in caves, rock crevices, hollow trees, or abandoned buildings. They keep their eggs sheltered from humans and other animals.

BREEDING SEASON
April brings showers—and the peak of turkey vulture breeding season! To attract a mate, turkey vultures might hop in a circle or flap and dive in the air. Most eggs are laid by June.

Turkey vulture eggs are large and cream-colored, with brown or lavender spots.

PERFECT PARENTING

Both turkey vulture parents take turns caring for the eggs. The chicks are helpless when they hatch. They're small, **downy**, and often blind. Both parents feed the chicks by **regurgitating** food.

LIFE CYCLE BY THE NUMBERS

1 to 3
Number of eggs laid

30 to 40 DAYS
Time for eggs to hatch

10-11 WEEKS
Time until chicks are independent

3 inches (7.6 cm)
Egg length

2 inches (5 cm)
Egg width

The Best Defense is...Vomit?

Like other wild animals, turkey vultures can face some dangerous situations from time to time. But don't worry—they've learned how to defend themselves.

KEEP YOUR DISTANCE!
Different animals have different ways to protect themselves from predators, but not many are as interesting as the turkey vulture's method of self-defense—they barf!

FLYING VOMIT
If a turkey vulture finds itself being bothered by another animal, it vomits right on them! Turkey vultures can send vomit up to 10 feet (3 m) in the air—that's about as high as a basketball hoop!

COZY KETTLE
Turkey vultures may also keep safe by forming a kettle. This is a group of vultures that travels in the air together.

Animals have many ways of keeping themselves safe. Let's see how these methods stack up against that of the turkey vulture!

Turtles hide by sneaking into their shells.

Skunks spray offenders with a sticky, foul-smelling liquid.

Bees sting their predators with a painful venom.

A threatened caterpillar curls into a ball.

An opossum plays dead to avoid an attack.

Battle of the Birds

One may be named after the other...but who would win the battle for most peculiar bird?

Mostly ground birds that stick to running. They fly short distances only.

"RIOT" WILD TURKEY

Found in North America and does not migrate

Listen for clucks and gobbles

Excellent eyesight—three times greater than a human's!

Chows down on seeds, nuts, grains, plants, and some insects or small reptiles

Turkey vultures soar across the sky 20,000 feet (6,096 m) above our heads. That's about two thirds as high as an airplane! That's very high...but there are still birds that can fly higher!

Andean condor
15,000 feet
(4,572 m)

White stork
16,000 feet
(4,876 m)

Turkey vulture
20,000 feet
(6,096 m)

VS

"THE TANK"
TURKEY VULTURE

Can fly and glide long distances

Found throughout North and South America, and migrate each year

Keen eyesight and a superb sense of smell

Love to feed on carrion of all kinds

Listen for grunts, whines, and hisses

40,000 ft

Ruppell's griffon vulture
37,000 feet (11,277 m)

35,000 ft

Crane
33,000 feet
(10,058 m)

30,000 ft

Bar-headed goose
29,000 feet
(8,839 m)

Whooper swan
27,000 feet
(8,229 m)

25,000 ft

Bearded vulture
24,000 feet
(7,315 m)

20,000 ft

15,000 ft

Fact or Fiction?

Turkey vultures are odd birds with a lot of unusual habits. Find which of these fun facts are true or false.

#1

Turkey vultures pee on themselves.

FACT!

When they get too hot, turkey vultures don't look for a lake to cool off—they pee on their legs instead!

#2

Turkey vultures have super strong legs.

FICTION!

Turkey vulture legs look a lot like chicken legs. That is why they depend on their super-sharp beak to cut up their dinner.

#3

Turkey vultures kill animals by dive-bombing them from the sky.

FICTION!

Turkey vultures don't kill their prey. They eat animals that are already dead!

#4

Turkey vultures prevent diseases from spreading.

FACT!

By eating dead animals before they decompose, turkey vultures prevent **bacteria** from growing and harming plants and other animals.

#5

A turkey vulture's vomit can kill bacteria.

FACT!

The digestive juices in a turkey vulture's stomach are strong enough to kill toxic bacteria. This is what allows them to eat carrion without getting sick.

#6

Turkey vultures circle dying animals, waiting to feed.

FICTION!

Turkey vultures soar in the air for hours on thermals, waiting to catch a whiff of a dead animal. They can smell carrion from miles away, but they cannot sense when an animal is dying.

Vulture Awareness

Turkey vultures are common birds and they're not currently at risk of dying out. Their biggest threat is actually humans!

HARM FROM HUMANS

Turkey vultures are often hit by cars, as they spend a lot of time near roads feeding on their favorite snack. They can also be killed by poisons and **pesticides** that were ingested by the animals they eat.

SUPER STOMACHS

Scientists at the Smithsonian National Museum of Natural History are studying how the bacteria in turkey vultures' stomachs can help destroy bad bacteria. This could prevent illness in humans and other animals!

SAY HELLO
Check the website of your nearest zoo to see if they have turkey vultures to visit. You might be able to watch their strange behaviors first-hand!

LOOK UP
If you live where turkey vultures are found, watch the sky and maybe you'll see a turkey vulture floating on a thermal!

You might not be able to see a turkey vulture vomit at a zoo, but you could see it eat dinner!

Learning More

BE A FRIEND TO TURKEY VULTURES

Turkey vultures circling in the sky might seem annoying or even creepy. And turkey vultures certainly deserve their reputation for being "gross" birds. But they are also grossly important! Other animals, including humans, need them to clean up their ecosystems.

Interested in turkey vulture conservation? Here are some important facts to know.

- Turkey vulture habitats are threatened by expanding human settlement and increased heat waves and fires caused by **global warming**.
- Turkey vultures prefer to spend their time away from humans. If you see one in the sky, it may be migrating or following the scent of a meal.
- Learn about how pesticides can contaminate an ecosystem and threaten the plants and animals that live there—including humans!

BOOKS

Gregory, Josh. *Vultures.* Scholastic, 2016.

Magellan, Marta. *Those Voracious Vultures.* Pineapple Press, 2008.

WEBSITES

Missouri Department of Conservation: Vulture Facts
https://mdc.mo.gov/wildlife/wildlife-facts/bird-facts/vulture-facts

All About Birds: Turkey Vulture
allaboutbirds.org/guide/Turkey_Vulture/overview

Chattahoochee Nature Center: 15 Interesting Facts About the Turkey Vulture
chattnaturecenter.org/visit/experience/wildlife/animal-facts/turkey-vulture/

Glossary

apex predators Predators, or animals that hunt and eat other animals, that are at the top of their food chain

bacteria Small, simple organisms that can be helpful, such as those that help digestion, or harmful, such as those that cause disease or infections

birds of prey Birds that hunt other animals for food

carcasses Dead bodies of animals

crevices Narrow openings, especially in rocks and walls

downy Covered with soft, fluffy feathers

energy The power or ability to do work

global warming The gradual warming of Earth's average temperature, due to human activity

lappets Folds or hanging pieces of flesh on animals

mature Fully grown or adult

migrations Regular movements from one place to another based on seasons

olfactory system The connected body parts that control the sense of smell

pesticides Substances meant to destroy pests

prey Animals that are eaten by other animals

range The area where a species is found

regurgitating Bringing food that has been swallowed back out of the mouth

ruff A ring of feathers or fur around an animal's neck

salvage Save something from being fully destroyed

scavengers Animals that feed on dead animals, plants, and garbage

species Groups of similar animals that can mate and reproduce with each other

thermals Upward currents of warm air formed when the surface of the ground is warmed by the Sun

toxins Poisonous substances

Comprehension Questions

1. _____ allow turkey vultures to glide for hours without flapping.
   a. Strong winds
   b. Thermals
   c. Clouds
2. On which continents are turkey vultures found?
   a. North and South America
   b. North America and Europe
   c. Europe and Asia
3. A turkey vulture's olfactory system is larger than in other birds. This gives it its incredible _____.
   a. Sense of smell
   b. Eyesight
   c. Flying ability
4. True or False: Turkey vultures have strong digestive juices that allow them to eat rotting flesh without getting sick.
5. True or False: Turkey vultures circle in the air above dying animals.

Answers: 1. B, 2. A, 3. A, 4. True, 5. False

Index

ABOUT THE AUTHOR

Samantha Kohn is a big fan of reading, writing, and traveling to places both near and far. This is her fourth children's book. Sam lives in London, Ontario, Canada with her husband, Steve. She loves coffee, sunshine, being on the water, and stopping to make friends with every dog she meets.

Crabtree Publishing

crabtreebooks.com   800-387-7650
Copyright © 2024 Crabtree Publishing

In Canada: We acknowledge the financial support of the Government of Canada through the Canada Book Fund for our publishing activities.

Hardcover   978-1-0398-1534-6
Paperback   978-1-0398-1560-5
Ebook (pdf)   978-1-0398-1612-1
Epub   978-1-0398-1586-5

Library and Archives Canada
Cataloguing in Publication
Available at the Library and Archives Canada

Library of Congress
Cataloging-in-Publication Data
Available at the Library of Congress

Published in Canada
Crabtree Publishing
616 Welland Avenue
St. Catharines, Ontario
L2M 5V6

Published in the United States
Crabtree Publishing
347 Fifth Avenue
Suite 1402-145
New York, NY 10016

Author: Samantha Kohn
Series research and development:
  Ellen Rodger, Janine Deschenes
Editorial director: Kathy Middleton
Editors: Ellen Rodger, Janine Deschenes
Proofreader: Crystal Sikkens
Design: Margaret Amy Salter

Images
Shutterstock: Daniel Bruce Lacy, p 29 (top)

All other images from Shutterstock

Printed in the U.S.A./072023/CG20230214